DON'T

GOSSIP

IN THE

TEACHERS'

LOUNGE

*150 Tips for
New Teachers*

REBECCA C. SCHMIDT

ROWMAN & LITTLEFIELD EDUCATION
A division of
ROWMAN & LITTLEFIELD PUBLISHERS, INC.
Lanham • New York • Toronto • Plymouth, UK

Published by Rowman & Littlefield Education
A division of Rowman & Littlefield Publishers, Inc.
A wholly owned subsidiary of
The Rowman & Littlefield Publishing Group, Inc.
4501 Forbes Boulevard, Suite 200, Lanham, Maryland 20706
www.rowmaneducation.com

Estover Road, Plymouth PL6 7PY, United Kingdom

British Library Cataloguing in Publication Information Available

Library of Congress Cataloging-in-Publication Data
Schmidt, Rebecca C.
    Don't gossip in the teachers' lounge : 150 tips for new teachers / Rebecca C.
Schmidt.
        p.   cm.
    ISBN 978-1-61048-657-6 (cloth : alk. paper)—ISBN 978-1-61048-658-3
(pbk. : alk. paper)—ISBN 978-1-61048-659-0 (electronic)
    1. First year teachers—United States—Handbooks, manuals, etc. 2. Teacher
effectiveness—United States—Handbooks, manuals, etc. 3. Teachers—
Employment—United States—Handbooks, manuals, etc. I. Title.
LB2844.1.N4S347 2012
371.1—dc23

                                                                2011044790

∞™ The paper used in this publication meets the minimum requirements of
American National Standard for Information Sciences—Permanence of Paper for
Printed Library Materials, ANSI/NISO Z39.48-1992.

Printed in the United States of America

This book is dedicated to Kathleen Percenti, one of the greatest teachers I have ever known. She was an elementary school teacher for forty years and is a hero to many, not only for the significant impact she made on young children but for the amazing person she is.

CONTENTS

Introduction   vii

Ethics   1

School Relationships   14

Parents   32

Professionalism   51

Child Dignity   73

Classroom Management   101

Media, Social Media, and Computers   119

Homework   129

Positive Learning Environment   137

About the Author   161

INTRODUCTION

From the time I was a small child, all I ever wanted was to become an elementary school teacher. I played school almost every day and had the smartest stuffed animals in the neighborhood.

I grew up with amazing role models who taught me the ins and outs of education on every level. My father was a clinical psychologist and a university professor. My mother taught middle school, high school, and was a school counselor. Education was a huge part of our lives.

I was a teacher for four years and decided to become an elementary school counselor. I have been an elementary school counselor for eighteen years.

While growing up, and during my twenty-three years in education, I learned tricks to help me become a more effective teacher and counselor. I have worked for fifteen principals (I have been responsible for counseling students at multiple schools in one district) and have worked with countless teachers and school employees. Over the years, I have seen how new teachers adapt to school life, the mistakes they have made, and the successes they have had.

It is my hope this book helps beginning elementary school teachers learn the inter-workings of school relationships, acquire classroom management strategies, learn effective parent communication techniques, gain knowledge of how to conduct themselves with the utmost professionalism, become aware of vital school ethics expectations, learn how to create a positive learning environment, and acquire an understanding of how imperative it is to preserve the dignity of each child at all costs.

Most of the tips you will read in this book are not taught in education classes in college but are learned through trial and error and only after years of experience.

ETHICS

The most important human endeavor is the striving for morality in our actions. Our inner balance and even our very existence depend on it. Only morality in our actions can give beauty and dignity to life.

—Albert Einstein

1.

Don't gossip in the teachers' lounge. News travels fast . . . the source of the news travels faster.

I have known teachers who are the "go-to" people to hear gossip. These teachers are known for spreading so much gossip that if you *want* information to spread, you go to them!

The problem is no one really respects that person! In a school, you want to be known as a professional who is trusted and looked up to. If you talk about kids, families, or other staff members, in the lounge, or anywhere, the news will get out that you are petty and not to be trusted. When someone begins to talk about a child in the lounge, just smile and change the subject as delicately as possible. A good line may be, "Oh, I don't want to interrupt your lunch by talking about that. Let's meet in your room after school and we can discuss it."

2.

Don't say anything to a child that you wouldn't say if their parents and their lawyer were in the room.

Have you ever heard the media report a story of a teacher saying something totally inappropriate, mean, or embarrassing to a child? Do you ever think, "Why on earth would a professional be so stupid?" Just make sure you are not one of those people! Parents are extremely protective of their children, as they should be, so if you say something demeaning or embarrassing to a child or in front of other children, the parents are going to march right up to the school to confront you and will possibly want everyone in the area to know how their child was treated! You will not have a leg to stand on when you are called in for the investigation. Remember to keep your cool and never put yourself in a position of question.

3.

Never, ever leave your students unattended. Just as your responsibility for them is continuous, so should be your attention.

There is never an excuse to leave your children without supervision. If you have to take an emergency bathroom break, tell the teacher next door to please watch your class or even call the office, but never take a chance. When teachers were in the bathroom or making copies, children have hurt each other, fallen from chairs and hit their heads, and so forth. This is a lawsuit waiting to happen, and no school district or union will protect you legally if the children were not supervised! Would you want your young child to be left alone in a room of twenty other young children? Neither do your students' parents.

4.

Always be honest and sincere. Children can detect dishonesty and insincerity a mile away.

The "singsongy" voice, the baby talk, etc., are equivalent to your Aunt Mary pinching your cheeks and squeezing you as hard as she can. Children get annoyed by this and find it unnerving. I know someone who speaks to children like this all the time and I heard one child say, "She is way too joyful and it makes me tired!"

Talk to children like they are important and let them know you think they are smart and capable. If you speak to them like they are babies, they may act like babies. Get on their level, look them in the eyes, and speak to them with respect no matter how old they are.

5.

Keep your eyes open for bruises or marks on a child and question the child about the origin.

If you are suspicious, tell your principal immediately and document *everything*! Do not depend on anyone else to report child abuse! Do not turn over a suspected child abuse claim to another and walk away. Tell the designated abuse reporter in your building, but it is your responsibility to sit in the room when a report is being made by the principal or school counselor and to obtain a copy of the report for your files. If your principal questions you about reporting an incident, take a stand! You do not want to be responsible for *not* reporting due to someone talking you out of it! If you see signs of abuse, *you need to report!* *It is the law!*

6.

Always do what you say you are going to do. Never let them down. They trust you.

Children need to be able to know what you say is accurate. If you say you are going to do something like take them outside for reading, then do it. If you say you are going to listen to a story they want to tell you after lunch, make sure you do it. Then, when something comes up that is not in the routine, they will trust you know what you are doing and they will feel safe and accept the change.

You remember adults in your life that may have promised you things and didn't follow through. It made you not trust them when they said anything. If you cannot trust an adult to follow through on small things, you cannot trust them with important things like feeling safe and secure around them. Do not leave them second-guessing things you say and wondering if you mean it.

7.

Always send a sick or injured child to the nurse regardless of how minor you think the problem is.

If a child says she feels like she is going to throw up or she hit her head or her arm hurts, send her to get it checked out by the nurse. Parents get furious if they feel their child is sick or hurt and you didn't let them get help. I have known children who fall on the playground and hurt their arm and two days later they come to school with a cast on it not knowing it was broken. If a child is consistently asking to go to the nurse, then of course, you have another issue you can discuss with the child's parent, the nurse, and the school counselor. These children may have issues with anxiety, bullying, problems at home, and so forth; they may actually feel "butterflies" in their stomach or have headaches or other symptoms they cannot fully explain. Even a child that seeks constant attention has issues and may need intervention.

8.

Do not lend or give children money for any reason.

If there is a book fair and the child is crying because he has no money, allow the child to call home, but do not give him money. This is not fair to all of the other children in your class. You can be very understanding and kind and help him cope with the disappointment, but do not offer to pay for something. This may happen at a gift shop on a field trip, for example. The only exception to this would be lunch money if your school does not have a lending policy. If a child will go without lunch unless you give her money, then lend her the money and write a note to the parents stating the child needs to bring in the amount of money the next day. Making a habit of lending money or buying extra things for a child can lead to problems.

9.

Do not believe what you hear about a child before he enters your class.

The child may have a horrible reputation, but give the child a chance before you make judgments about him or her. It may be that the last teacher had a personality conflict with the child or that the child was going through a difficult year at home due to family issues. You want the children to give you a chance to get to know you, so give them a fair chance to get to know them.

Children know they have a reputation. They know what people in the school think of them. They hear people talking; they know children stay away from them; they know adults in the school think they are "bad" and they get blamed for lots of things for which they may or may not be responsible. Be one of those people that sees the good in them. Make them believe there is good in them. They will rise to the occasion.

10.

You are an upstanding citizen in your community. You were hired to do a job and to represent your school district.

Do not go to area bars and drink alcohol or act like a teenager when you are out with your friends. Yes, it is your time and you should be able to do whatever you want to do, but you can't when you are in the school neighborhood and you can easily run into parents and children. If you want to socialize and drink, choose a place far from the school district.

I have known colleagues who go to school fund-raisers with administrators, parents, and colleagues and act like it is a fraternity or sorority party. They use it as an excuse to drink a lot and party; they forget it is a school function, even if it is on a weekend night and at a party center. Having a glass of wine, dancing, and laughing is appropriate. Getting loud and drunk and making a scene could come back to haunt you on Monday morning.

Also, remember, if you are caught drinking and driving, you could lose your teaching license and it is simply not worth it!

11.

There is never any reason to divulge confidential information to other colleagues about a specific child unless that colleague is directly involved with that child and the information is shared to help the child succeed.

There is never a reason to divulge confidential information to another child's parent! If you are going to speak about a child, make sure it is very positive. You never know with whom you are sharing information. It could be the child's distant cousin or the child's neighbor. It is always a good idea to avoid talking about school-related issues at all if you are at the grocery store or the community pool. You never know who will overhear a conversation.

Don't ever put yourself in a situation where you walk away from a conversation and worry whether or not you said too much or whether certain information you shared will get back to the child or their family.

12.

Do not share information about a child with any family members other than the custodial parents.

Well-meaning grandmas and grandpas and aunts and uncles may want to know how little David is doing. When you are asked these questions, answer with a generic phrase such as, "He is such a helpful little boy," or "He has such good manners." Anything else is a breach of confidentiality. You never know what the relationship is between the child's parents and these other relatives and you do not want to get in the middle of this situation. Many times, it is very innocent and everything about the child is shared between the parents and grandparents, but you should not do the sharing!

SCHOOL RELATIONSHIPS

When we seek to discover the best in others, we
somehow bring out the best in ourselves.

—William Arthur Ward

13.

Always compliment teacher-aides, office personnel, bus drivers, and other staff on their hard work. With very little effort, you can become a very positive force in the life of your school.

Unfortunately, these professionals are treated "less-than" by some and many times work the hardest in the school! I have heard children say, "I don't have to listen to you. You're not a teacher!" Of course, this should *never* be tolerated, and the child should have a consequence and be required to write an apology letter to the adult he insulted. These professionals should be treated with the utmost respect just as you expect others to treat you. Give them compliments and tell them they are doing a great job by writing them a little note. If you hear someone say something positive about them, make sure to share the compliment with them!

If you disagree with any adult in the school, never do it in front of children! This makes you look unprofessional and undermines the other adult. This will get back to the administrator and probably will be shared at the dinner table by the children who heard you.

14.

Become friends with the school secretary and the custodians because they run the school.

These personnel, among others, are vital contributors to the running of the school. The secretaries know most of the behind-the-scenes workings of the entire school and can help you tremendously if you have questions. The custodian has an extremely important job regarding the safety and the maintenance of the building. These two people can help you in a crisis and are important colleagues. However, they are very busy. Please remember they are dealing with students, staff, and parents all day and you are just one person who needs help during their day. Do not ask them questions you can figure out on your own and do not have the custodian do anything you can do on your own like hang a picture or move a desk.

15.

Never be late taking your children to art, music, gym, library, the cafeteria, or other such places. Your tardiness affects many others.

If you are finishing up a phone call or an e-mail during your planning time and are late to pick up your students, they are *unattended*. It is not the responsibility of the art, music, or gym teachers to babysit while they are supposed to be teaching their next class. Everyone is on a tight schedule, so do not make it hard on your colleagues. You may know how this feels if you have experienced a conference night where you have back-to-back parent conferences scheduled and one parent is even five minutes late. The tardiness affects many other people. If this tardiness becomes a habit, your colleagues *will* let your principal know, and you will more than likely be called into a meeting with the principal.

16.

Be extremely flexible.

Faculty, staff, parents, or students do not like a rigid teacher. Rigidity sometimes serves only to protect you or punish others.

I have known teachers who just "go with the flow." Usually, these teachers are easy to get along with and are chosen for special committees, among other things. Administrators want to accommodate these teachers more when the teacher asks for a favor because they have made the principal's life easier by "going with the flow." Therefore, the principal usually wants to return the favor.

Rigid, inflexible teachers are those who express anger or annoyance when a small change in the schedule is needed or when their day doesn't go as planned. These teachers usually come across as grumpy, hard to work with, unhappy, and passive-aggressive. It seems everything is always about them and not about what is best for the children or best for the school. These are the teachers who students, colleagues, and parents are eager to see retire.

17.

On the birthdays of the principal, secretaries, custodians, and other personnel, let your students write letters or draw pictures.

At the beginning of the year, ask a colleague if there is a staff birthday list posted anywhere. If there isn't, ask the secretary if she has a copy of the staff birthdays.

This writing assignment could be a morning routine such as morning work. You can create a template of a formal letter on the board and have the children fill in the template. On the board, you could write:

Today, someone special in our school is having a birthday! It is Mrs. Langley. Please write a nice letter and tell her what you like best about her.

For fun, you could choose the child with the closest birthday to that day as the delivery person. Don't forget to let the children with summer birthdays deliver the first or last ones of the year.

Some other suggestions include: putting sample letters or key phrases in a writing center for the students to use or getting a big piece of bulletin board paper and making a giant birthday card with everyone writing or drawing something on it.

This activity teaches children to think of others. Children like to be remembered, appreciated, and special—adults are no different.

18.

Don't bother your principal
unless it is necessary.

You think your job is hard. Write down your questions, put them on her desk, and let her come to you when she has time. Make sure no one else—an experienced teacher, the secretary, the custodian, or the school counselor, for example—can answer those questions.

There are three basic reasons a new teacher initiates contact with a principal:

- To inform the principal of a situation that is beyond the control of the teacher.
- To inform the principal of a situation that may have significant repercussions and therefore must be reported.
- To try to curry favor and/or establish a social relationship with the principal.

As busy as she may be, the principal always has time for the first two listed above, but she is much too busy for the third reason.

19.

Don't ask the school secretary to do anything you can do for yourself, like type a letter.

She is probably the busiest person at the school.

School secretaries can be the most underappreciated staff at the school. Usually, they are so efficient that they make the job look easy and effortless. It isn't!

The school secretary has to do lunch counts, attendance, report card organization, and cumulative folder organization. She must order supplies, answer the phone, schedule meetings, play interference for the principal and teachers, field numerous calls from parents, coordinate substitutes, etc., etc. Also, she answers a thousand questions a day and does all of these things with constant interruption.

You can type your own letter.

20.

Place a good news note in a colleague's mailbox if you see them doing something above and beyond and tell them you noticed.

Imagine coming to work one morning and finding a note from a colleague in your mailbox telling you he passed your room and saw an amazing lesson you were teaching or how he really admired how you handled a difficult situation in a meeting. You would appreciate that small gesture so much and you would remember it every time you see that person.

If you see an instructional assistant doing a great job working with a student or helping a child overcome an obstacle, write her a note telling her how lucky that child is to have her. If you see the lunch aide helping a child find their lost money, write a little note letting him know how nice it was and how you really appreciate working with such great people. If you see the custodian working hard to set up for an assembly, tell him how much you notice and appreciate his hard work.

21.

Don't be a pain to the custodians!

Clean up your room and let the children help you! Explain to the children how the custodians have many, many rooms to clean every night so the school looks neat and clean the following school day.

Ask the custodian to come into your room at the beginning of the year and talk about his job. Have him tell the children how many rooms need to be cleaned, how many garbage cans need to be emptied, and how many floors need vacuuming every day. Ask the children to imagine each classroom is their bedroom and ask them how they would feel having to clean many rooms every day. This will let them know how important it is to keep their classroom clean to make it easier for the custodians.

22.

Have the lunch monitors and recess monitors visit your classroom at the beginning of the year and explain to your students how important their jobs are.

Explain to the children they are responsible for everyone getting and eating their lunch, cleaning up their messes, and being safe on the playground. Remind the students these adults deserve just as much respect as the classroom teachers in the building. During this visit, tell the children the principal chose these people to monitor the children in the lunchroom and at recess because they were the best qualified for the position. Let the students know these important people are responsible for many, many children and want to keep everyone safe and healthy and they want everyone to have a fun recess.

23.

Go to the dollar store and purchase a number of birthday cards.

Keep these cards on hand at school and put them in the mailboxes of your colleagues on their birthdays. It is a nice touch and truly appreciated. Don't you appreciate it when someone remembers your birthday?

If you know they drink coffee or a specific soft drink, take it to their classroom first thing in the morning before the children arrive.

It takes so little to make someone's day and to let them know you are thinking of them.

24.

Ask if you can help the social committee plan school events.

Usually, there is a social committee who is responsible for purchasing flowers for a teacher who has had a new baby or for an employee who is in the hospital. In addition, this committee plans luncheons for the staff, sends cards, purchases presents for the principal on special occasions, purchases a gift for the secretary for Secretaries' Day, etc. Most often, dues are collected at the beginning of the school year to cover these purchases. If you are on this committee, you will get to know people and learn what is going on around the school.

When on a committee, you will get to know the staff, but they will also get to know you so make sure you follow their lead at first and be as helpful as possible. Share ideas, but do not be demanding or critical of their ideas. At first, simply do what is needed to make the committee a success and make sure the other team members know you are willing to help in any way.

25.

Share ideas with your grade-level colleagues.

If you have an idea, put copies of the idea in their mailboxes. Do not hog ideas or keep them for your own. Doing this only makes the other teachers feel you are not a team player and you are trying to upstage them. If they choose not to do the activity or lesson, that is fine, but at least you offered the idea to them.

I have known teachers who think of a great idea and the only time their teammates know about the idea is when they are getting lots of attention from parents or administrators and are "grandstanding." Their colleagues felt they were left out and felt the new teacher was trying to get attention and leaving them behind. Just make sure you share your ideas and even ask your colleagues for their input. If you ask their advice, they will feel you are including them and not hiding something from them. If they have a great idea for you, make sure to give them credit and let them know you did.

26.

Do not talk about one team member to other members.

Even if they begin to talk or gossip, leave the room, sit silently, etc. If a colleague or parent talks about another teacher, just try to change the subject or say something like, "Wow, that doesn't sound like her," or "I have never had that experience when dealing with her."

You work in an environment where gossip can be over-whelming sometimes. Do not get caught up in this gossip and do not be worried about what you have said when you leave a conversation. Just be safe and don't say anything negative.

You are the new kid on the block. Whatever you say will spread and if you talk about one team member, the others will think you will eventually talk about them.

27.

Don't forget to acknowledge crossing guards and bus drivers at your school.

Some morning, arrive early and take the crossing guard a donut and coffee or hand the bus driver a $5 gift card to a donut shop. Go to the dollar store and buy a pair of gloves and hand them to the crossing guard one morning with a note saying how much you appreciate her. These small gestures will mean so much and will let them know how much you value them and the job they perform.

Can you imagine driving eighty young children around twice a day and dealing with discipline, bullying, rowdiness, screaming, eating on the bus, etc., and concentrating on morning traffic all at the same time? Not to mention parents who walk their children to the bus and complain about something that happened on the bus or just want to talk as the bus driver is trying to stay on schedule.

Crossing guards and bus drivers get up at the crack of dawn in all kinds of weather and do their job. These colleagues are very underappreciated and should be recognized.

28.

Ask your principal if you can provide a snack at a staff meeting once in a while.

Throw some hard candy or chocolate in the middle of the tables at a staff meeting or get pretzels and plastic cups and let the teachers fill up their cups on the way into the meeting. These little gestures are appreciated, especially after school when everyone is hungry and tired.

These small gestures will make you a positive force in your school. If you help make others have an easier or more pleasant day, it will make your days pleasant and they will return the favor. It takes very little to make a huge difference in the lives of others.

29.

Be the solution to problems.

If you complain about something or detect a problem in the school, don't bring it up unless you have a possible solution. For example, if children leave their coats and gloves all over the playground after recess, maybe you can bring this up and suggest a class clothes monitor scans the playground before they come into the building. Just have a solution with your problem. If students are leaving their tables dirty after lunch, assign a cleanup crew to help the lunch monitors.

Be the solution to a problem. If someone doesn't show up first thing in the morning due to traffic, offer to watch their class until they arrive by combining your class with theirs. If it is your planning time and you are needed somewhere in the building to watch a class or help out in the office, do it with a smile. No, this is not something you want to do all of the time and you do not want others to take advantage of your flexibility and kindness; however, even if the solution is rejected or doesn't work out, at least you will not be known as a complainer but as a problem solver.

PARENTS

Making the decision to have a child is momentous. It is to decide forever to have your heart go walking around outside your body.

—Elizabeth Stone

30.

During a parent conference, be very calm and kind. The parents are more nervous than you are.

You are going into a room, possibly with other professionals, to critique every aspect of the person who means more to the parents than life itself! Even if you are having a difficult time with this child, remember to be calm and kind. This is a perfect time to put yourself in the parents' shoes and imagine sitting and listening to someone evaluate and critique you or your child in front of others. Parents feel children are a direct reflection of themselves. If you say something mean, uncaring, or negative about their child, you are saying it about them!

31.

Always start a parent conference with something positive about the child. In a conference, the parents are in unfamiliar, and frequently, they suspect, unfriendly territory. Let them know they are key members of the teaching team and you respect them.

You would not have a job if it weren't for parents and their children. Unfortunately, some teachers feel a conference is the time to let the parents know all of the things that are wrong with the child and it is the teacher's "duty" to be direct and honest. If you have something to say that is a weakness of the child's, accompany it with a solution. If the child has a difficult time organizing, tell this to the parents and say you are going to try to help the child by teaching her how each paper has a home and to place each loose paper in the correct home like the science folder home, the take-home folder home, etc. Have a solution! It is your job to teach the child learning strategies and work skills, not to lay a lot of problems on the parents to work out.

32.

Always end a parent conference with something positive about the child.

Sometimes, new teachers feel it is their obligation to point out the child's shortcomings, difficulties, weaknesses, and mistakes. However, keep in mind that anyone can criticize a child and, generally, you are not telling the parents anything they already do not know. Just be kind when being truthful.

Imagine yourself shopping for a bathing suit and coming out of the dressing room to be critiqued by models, bathing suit manufacturers, and other fashion professionals. You probably would feel embarrassed, exposed, and self-conscious. It would help if those professionals would tell you the parts they like and give you ideas on how they were going to help you look better rather than pick apart each detail. You would also want them to end on a positive! Parents in a conference feel exposed and self-conscious because, again, they feel their child is a direct reflection of themselves. End the conference positively!

33.

Write or e-mail positive notes home to parents at least once a week.

All of us welcome positive communication, and nothing is more welcoming to a parent than a positive comment about their child. Make sure when parents see an e-mail or message from you they don't automatically dread it.

Let parents know if their child says something cute or funny. Parents love to hear these comments and appreciate you taking the time to let them know. Parents wish they could be with their children as much as you are and they love to hear funny things their young children say in their absence so they feel they haven't missed anything.

If you frequently are sending positive communication, when you have bad news, parents will be more receptive.

34.

Call parents at home in August and tell them how pleased you are to have their child in your class.

This establishes you as a different type of teacher and establishes the beginning of a relationship. This positive relationship will help you throughout the year.

You will have a class list by the first day you arrive after the summer, but you may want to go to the school and ask if you can have a copy a few days before teachers return and write down the phone numbers of your students. Call each home and leave a message that you are David's new teacher and you are so excited to have him in your class. Tell the family on the answering machine about how much fun you are going to have in second grade this year and you cannot wait until the first day of school to meet David!

Each call should not take more than one to two minutes, which means you will spend roughly thirty to forty-five minutes on this task. This small amount of time spent will help you begin your positive relationship with this family and this child even before the child enters your classroom.

35.

If you have a child in your class whose parents are divorced, make sure you look in the child's cumulative folder to see the divorce agreement.

If they have shared parenting, this means you are to send all information to both parents. You can ask your school secretary for the school's specific policy, but make sure you check.

Some parents may request copies of report cards and progress reports but do not have custody of the child at all; it is up to the custodial parent to pass these along. Some agreements say all educational information goes to both parents. Read the document carefully and follow it.

36.

If you have a child in your class whose parents are divorced, make sure you are very clear as to whom you can release the child to.

Even though a child knows his/her daddy, it does not mean he has a legal right to take the child from school. Ask the school secretary if there are any restrictions on the release of a child to a parent in a divorce situation and look in the cumulative folder to read the divorce agreement. The school office gets these documents and knows who can be released to whom, but make sure you know!

37.

Do not jump to conclusions if a parent does not seem involved in the child's school life.

If a parent cannot make a conference or arrives late, if she does not immediately respond to e-mails or phone calls, if permission slips aren't turned in on time, or if homework is not checked over at home, there could be a number of reasons. This parent may be single and struggling to survive. He may have multiple jobs and is more concerned about providing a roof over the child's head and having food on the table than about turning in twenty-five pipe cleaners for a project.

Help out that parent as much as possible. Ask her what you can do to make her life easier. Maybe it is giving the child a little more time to complete a project or giving the child class time to do it while using your supplies.

38.

Do not require children to bring lots of things for projects that cost money.

Five dollars may be a fortune to some families who live from paycheck to paycheck and it may be right before payday. Appropriate items to ask for may be things they can easily find around their house like a magazine, paper plates, or a shoebox. If it has to be something from a store, maybe you should change your project. If you are doing color days and expect a child to wear something red, for example, make sure you give them an alternative like making a red name tag out of construction paper and pinning it on instead of wearing a red shirt. This way the child and the parents can save face if the child does not own a shirt that is that specific color.

39.

Make sure all of the correspondence you send to parents is spelled correctly and grammatically correct!

Pretend the superintendent and the principal will be reading the e-mail or the newsletter you are sending, because you never know when they may be. Your written communication should always be of very high quality even if it is a simple thank-you note.

Unfortunately, I have seen classroom newsletters go home to parents with missing capital letters and punctuation and run-on sentences. Most parents notice everything. How can you expect to be looked at as a professional who is a positive role model to children when your communication with parents and the community is sloppy and incorrect? Proofread *everything* that goes home at least two times.

40.

Do not make friends with the parents of your students unless their child is out of your class.

This may be difficult and it may sound counterproductive, but it is not professional to socialize with parents, communicate with them on social networking sites, or become friendly enough to contact them in the evenings or on weekends just to talk.

The child is your priority and it may be difficult to communicate honestly with a parent with whom you have become very friendly. You may have to discuss behavioral issues, learning issues, social issues, etc., and your friendship could get in the way of what is best for the child. Other parents will become aware of this relationship and could think you are favoring your friend's child over theirs. Be very kind, but always be professional.

41.

Parents are wonderful volunteers in the classroom, but make sure to set boundaries.

If the same parents want to volunteer all the time, give them a specific time and day of the week, but let all interested parents have an opportunity. Do not favor one over the other, even though you may want to.

Children act differently when their parents are around. If the child of the volunteer misbehaves, have a private conversation with the parent and the child and let the child know the behavior needs to stop or the parent will no longer be allowed to volunteer.

Parents can take small groups of children in the hall to work on math facts, they can stuff envelopes or mailboxes, they can help with art projects, etc. Make sure they do not see confidential information like the report cards, grades, or parent communication of the other children.

Of course, make sure you never share confidential information with a parent or confide in a parent hoping they won't spread the information. Most likely, they will.

42.

If you are doing a project for Mother's Day, Father's Day, or Valentine's Day, for example, make sure you include grandparents and special loved ones.

Children who have lost a parent or do not have contact with a parent can dread these projects.

One idea may be to have a "spring project" they can take home on the Friday before Mother's Day so they do not have to feel like they have to give it to anyone. This way, if they choose to give it to their mom or grandmother they can, but it is not a Mother's Day present.

Some teachers simply choose not to do these activities if they have a child who has lost a parent or has an absent parent. Others feel this is like punishing the children who have not experienced this loss. This will be something you will have to decide depending on your students' circumstances, but just be aware of these issues when you begin these projects.

43.

During orientation, tell the parents you will believe 50 percent of what their children tell you about their lives at home if they believe 50 percent of what the child says about their life at school.

Remind the parents children are viewing the world through their seven-year-old brains. Many times, the child perceives other children and adults in a much different light than adults; therefore, parents need to take this into consideration when listening to a child's story. Encourage parents to contact you for the whole story before jumping to conclusions.

Tell the parents you will hear details about their lives, but you will not take those as absolute truths as long as they do not take what they hear about school as the absolute truth. Stories get very distorted and are usually told with the child being innocent. Many times, these stories are not meant to be dishonest, but they are filtered through the child's eyes.

44.

At the beginning of the year, have each child draw a picture of their family and write about the fun things they do together.

Save these in a safe place. Have them do this at the end of the school year as well. Get a big piece of construction paper and glue the first one on the left side of the paper and the second one on the right side. Write the date the child drew these under each picture. Give this to the family at the end of the school year. It is a precious keepsake and it will show the parents the wonderful progress the child has made throughout the year.

45.

There are going to be some parents you just cannot please.

They will question every remark you make, every paper you send home, and every project you do. It is best just to deal with these parents just like all of the others. Be very kind and professional. Set boundaries and be straightforward and to the point when dealing with these parents.

Some parents will threaten to tell the principal or superintendent. Do not feel intimidated by this. There is no need to constantly defend yourself, but you can share a simple reason for doing what you did by referring to the curriculum or explaining your grading procedures, for example. Some parents feel they need to show you they are in control by criticizing you. Just remember, their issues are not truly about you and they will do this to the child's future teachers as well.

46.

Parents with elementary-school-aged children sometimes have a difficult time hearing negative things about their children.

It is very difficult for parents to hear their child may have a learning disability or social/emotional issues. They probably have heard the news in little pieces before from preschool teachers, other parents, or family members, but they are not ready to accept the information. They will go into defense mode. They may blame you or others; they may say you are picking on their child; they may say the child performs very well at home and it must be the school's fault the child is not performing at school.

The best way to deal with these parents is to have empathy and be kind and understanding. This is their most prized possession you are talking to them about. Their worst fear is to hear something negative that could impact the child's life or happiness. Gather data to show your concerns. Elicit help from your school psychologist or school counselor, but make sure you have contacted the parents with your concerns before you bring in others. Parents will feel bombarded and attacked if they walk into a parent conference with a room full of educational experts. Make sure they know you are gathering people to come up with a plan the whole *team* (which includes the parents, of course) agrees with. Make sure they know your goal is exactly the same for their child—to be successful, healthy, and happy.

47.

Tell parents at orientation you will not believe one child over another.

Explain to them that if a situation occurs and a child does not admit to breaking a rule or an adult does not see it, you will not believe one child over another. Follow this with every situation. Even if a child who is constantly breaking rules gets into a problem with a child who never gets into trouble, do not just assume the troublemaker is at fault. Explain this to parents at the beginning of the year and explain you would not take another child's word over their child's.

PROFESSIONALISM

A professional is someone who can do his best work when he doesn't feel like it.

—Alistair Cooke

48.

Try to handle your own issues in your classroom before seeking help.

Perhaps the greatest difference between an experienced, mature teacher and a new teacher is knowledge of the level at which a problem should be solved—when the teacher alone should deal with it, when to call parents, and when to call the counselor, the principal, or other personnel.

There are some teachers who forget how many children are in the school! Most elementary schools have roughly five hundred students. If you are known as the teacher who can't solve any of your own problems, you will become a nuisance to the other professionals in the building. For example, keep Band-Aids in your desk. They are peeled off easily and it saves on trips to the nurse's office. The school nurse is dealing with diabetic children, children with asthma, distributing medication, etc., and sending a child down to the clinic to get a Band-Aid, or to treat a headache that could be cured with a wet paper towel in the classroom, does not make sense.

The counselor is busy dealing with children experiencing a divorce, bullying issues, parent issues, behavioral issues, etc. Sending a child down to the counselor to work out a simple recess friendship issue is a waste of the counselor's time. Have the children take five minutes after recess and discuss the situation and what *they* are going to do to help them solve their own issue.

Have you ever seen a principal with nothing to do? Usually not! Every time you peek your head into the principal's office and say, "Do you have a second?," remember that twenty people have already done that the same day! Experience will help you learn when a situation is handled by you, and when it should be handled by another school professional. Use the adage, "Ask Three Before Me." Ask a few veteran teachers whom you respect what to do.

Then, when you do approach the principal about a problem, she will drop everything to listen because she will know it must be very important if you are bringing it to her attention!

49.

Never become distracted during recess. Trouble takes only a few seconds. Remember, it's your students' recess, not yours.

In some schools, teachers are responsible for monitoring their students at recess. In other schools, the grade levels have a teacher assigned to recess once a week and they rotate the supervision. Yet in other schools, aides are hired to monitor recess.

If you are a recess monitor, make sure your eyes are on all parts of the playground and you are not distracted from your duties. You do not want a child to fall off of a slide or a scuffle to break out because you were reading a book while sitting on a bench or discussing weekend plans with another teacher.

50.

Don't sit at your desk when your students are working. They aren't there to watch you grade papers.

Your school district pays you to teach children. When the children are in your classroom, you should be monitoring their learning and progress all of the time.

Giving children worksheets to do and then doing paperwork is not teaching. If the students are completing worksheets, this is a good time for you to be meeting with small reading or math groups at a back table, or walking around monitoring the students' independent work, but not writing e-mails or grading papers.

51.

Never grade papers during a staff meeting.

Keep eye contact with the principal. It's a matter of respect. For some reason, teachers seem to be the worst at keeping quiet during meetings or conferences. Many feel this is a time for them to socialize or get paperwork completed. Some teachers even roll their eyes or laugh or gossip while in a staff meeting.

Principals know this and become frustrated when teachers do not pay attention in staff meetings or to a speaker the district has brought in for staff development. This is very unprofessional and disrespectful. If you want to be treated as a professional, act like a professional. Look in the principal's eyes when she is speaking. The respect will be noted and returned.

52.

Always listen carefully and take notes during a faculty meeting.

As a new teacher, you can't always tell which information is important and which is not. Always listen carefully and take notes during a faculty meeting.

Most principals do not like staff meetings any more than teachers do, but this is their opportunity to share things they need to communicate to you about the school and the district. Principals attend meetings with other administrators and the superintendent on a regular basis and they are responsible for sharing that information with their staff. In addition, the principal will share policy and procedural changes at the building level. Some of this information will need to be shared by you with your students and their parents. Take notes!

53.

Keep every handout you get at a faculty meeting and in your teacher's box in a binder. You will need them later.

Just make it a habit of having a binder separated by school year where you keep all handouts you get at staff meetings and in your teacher's box so you will be able to refer back to them if needed.

You will receive things like schedules, policies, procedures, school-wide rules, committee opportunities, and so on. Don't ever say you did not get something when, in reality, you lost it. This is part of your reputation as a professional.

54.

Stay in control of your emotions.

You have been around people who lose control of their emotions. If it happens often, it is like being close to a balloon and not knowing when it is going to pop. You are always leery and on edge waiting for the next outburst. Adults who "pop" with anger are seen as being out of control, hotheaded, and immature.

Whenever you get upset with a student, a colleague, an administrator, a secretary, in a faculty meeting or in a parent conference, people stop listening to what you are saying and react solely to the emotion they are hearing.

55.

Never say negative things to another teacher about your students. Would you want your child's teacher to talk about your child?

As a new teacher, you do not know who knows what family or who is related to whom. Not only is it extremely unethical and unprofessional to speak negatively about a child, it is also a good way to get into trouble with the principal and won't gain you any friends.

The principal may hear about the gossip and many may agree with it, but you may be called in to discuss your professionalism. In addition, you don't know whether that child's aunt is the principal's cousin or a colleague's best friend. Just play it safe and do not speak negatively or gossip about any child. Remember, never say anything about a child you would not say if their parents and lawyer were sitting right there!

56.

Never raise your voice. The louder you talk, the less people listen.

The more emotion in your voice, the less people concentrate on what you have to say. To get undivided attention, drop your voice. This advice is true in the classroom, in a meeting, or speaking to an irate parent or colleague.

I have known well-respected teachers who have gotten so flustered with a yelling parent, they began trying to yell louder. I also have seen teachers sit calmly as they are being berated and hold it together until the parent is finished. Then, they calmly begin talking or calmly walk over and buzz the office for an administrator. If you scream and yell, people will listen to the emotion you are spewing and not the words you are saying. If you remain calm, you will be respected and admired for your composure in a tough situation.

57.

Never argue with a child; you will lose every time.

When you begin negotiating or arguing with a child, you have lost control. Simply say, "I care about you too much to argue with you." This statement will, more than likely, defuse the situation.

Never tell a child "shut up" or lose control when speaking with a student. If you keep your voice calm and steady, you will keep yourself in control. Have you ever heard the noises the adults make on the *Peanuts* cartoons? The "wah, wah, wah . . ." is what the children hear after the first few words of a tirade. They block out everything you are saying and are just listening to yelling. The second you lose control of your emotions, you have lost the battle!

Children have a great way of catching you off guard or pushing buttons you didn't even know you had. You may find yourself arguing with a seven-year-old who has a pretty good reason not to do what you have just asked her to do so you may begin to defend your reasoning for asking her to do it! Then, she will find more reasons to argue because she feels she is "breaking you down" since you are now in the defensive mode. Yes, even three- and four-year-olds can do this!

58.

Never talk about your principal behind his back. It will *always* get back to him sooner or later.

It is human nature. People like to be the bearers of important news. It doesn't matter whether the news is good or bad, but that it is just news. Sometimes, it doesn't even have to be news that is true.

If a colleague feels at all insecure, he could be one of these people who cannot wait to share any news about the boss with others. Do not trust that if you simply say, "Let's keep this between us," or "Don't let this leave this room," that it won't! Principals know everything that is going on in the building! So does central office. As stated previously, news travels fast and the source travels faster!

59.

Volunteer to be on at least two school or district committees a year.

This will give you greater insight into the workings, personalities, and complexity of the operations of your school district. If you are on a committee, make sure you complete all of your committee assignments on time.

Just as committee work gives you an opportunity to see others from a different perspective, keep in mind they too are getting an opportunity to form opinions of you.

60.

Always look your best. Remember, you are a role model.

Make sure you read the student handbook and you follow their dress code as well as the employee handbook. If it says no flip-flops, don't wear flip-flops.

Many schools have spirit day or dress-down day on Fridays. This does not mean you wear old jeans and ratty tennis shoes. This simply means you do not dress up like you usually do Monday through Thursday and you are permitted to wear more casual attire.

Some of your colleagues will not follow this "always look your best" policy. Ignore that. This does not mean you are supposed to copy them. You do not have to wear suits and heels, but business attire is always preferred.

Dress like you will be running into the superintendent every day. You never know when you will.

61.

Try not to curse at home. It makes it easier not to slip at school.

Cursing includes saying things like "this sucks," "crap," and "Jesus Christ!"

Yes, I know you want to curse sometimes and it is warranted; but if you ever slip, you will, most likely, be written up by your principal. Yes, she will find out! So will parents. You will be the main topic at the dinner table that evening if you curse in front of children. That news will travel like wildfire!

62.

Eat a good breakfast. You will need the energy.

Sometimes, children may mistake your tiredness for a lack of interest in them. If you don't eat breakfast, by mid-morning, you are going to get tired, lethargic, and possibly irritable. Eating breakfast is an easy way to combat this. If you have a snack time in your classroom or a break in the mornings, bring some nuts or fruit for a pick-me-up.

63.

When you begin teaching, buy a box of manila file folders.

Whenever you have an article or an activity you find in a book or magazine, put it in a file and label it with, say, "Attention Deficit Disorder" or maybe "Community Helper Lessons." This prevents lost articles and piles of great ideas all over your desk that you may lose or throw away.

In a year or two, you will have a wonderful resource for yourself. I did that twenty-three years ago and have extensive files that I refer to often.

64.

Never go over your principal's head to central office.

If you have a curriculum question, a standardized testing question, etc., ask other teachers, ask the school psychologist or school counselor, or ask the secretary. If they do not know, ask the principal, but do not ever call central office unless you are instructed to by the principal. Some principals consider this to be going behind their back. Some feel it makes them look bad to their bosses and that they cannot handle their own building issues.

I have known colleagues who feel they can communicate with their boss's boss whenever they would like to and complain or ask questions. Remember, you have twenty-five students and parents to deal with. The principal has five hundred students and parents. Central office has over a thousand. Your question or issue can wait or can be handled on a lower level.

65.

Always be on time.

This sounds so simple and so obvious, but to some teachers, it is not. Principals know everything. When you come in the back door fifteen minutes late, they will find out. Believe it or not, some of your colleagues may mention it or the principal may need you to speak to a parent in the office and they will call your name over the PA system.

That can be embarrassing because then everyone knows you are not there. It is even worse if you have children in your classroom unattended and you are not there! If one gets hurt, the school district will not be able to defend you. Of course, things happen and traffic issues develop, weather issues arise, and so forth. When that happens occasionally, make sure you call the office to let them know so they can assign someone to watch your class until you arrive.

66.

Don't talk to the principal about your colleagues unless it is an emergency and a child is being hurt emotionally or physically.

The principal does not have time to hear idle gossip or time to hear what you think your colleagues are doing wrong. It is very possible the news will get back to your colleagues and, remember, you possibly have to work with these people for the rest of your career.

I have known colleagues who tattle on the staff for various reasons. If you are known for this, you will not have many friends at all and when you enter the principal's office, she will secretly roll her eyes and think, "Here we go again."

67.

Don't try to outdo your colleagues.

Don't try to one-up them by putting on elaborate displays or having big performances for parents to show off. Does this mean not to do your best or not to be creative? Not at all. If you have a great idea, share it with your teammates. If they want to do it, great! If not, then at least you have offered. If you exclude them or try to look better than them, you will accomplish the opposite.

CHILD DIGNITY

They may forget what you said, but they will
never forget how you made them feel.

—Carol Buchner

68.

Don't let children pick their teams. It helps prevent hurt feelings.

Yes, part of childhood is getting hurt feelings, but why set up a situation that is avoidable? Children are children, and they will choose friends to be on their teams and they will not choose kids that their friends don't like. So this social order is being put on display in front of the entire class when you have them choose their own teams. Pick numbers out of a hat, break up the alphabet, separate according to birthdays, but do not allow children to pick their own teams.

69.

Assign a different child to water your plants weekly. You may forget, but they won't.

Children love to please adults and giving them important jobs in the classroom lets them know they must be special if you are depending on them to do the job. Giving them jobs also reinforces their self-help skills and teaches them to think of others. All of this builds their self-esteem. Also, these tasks will definitely get done and you can relax a little.

70.

Make a bulletin board for the children to display their work. They love it and it is less work for you.

Children love to see their work displayed whether it is on their refrigerator at home or in the classroom. Having a special bulletin board just to display nice work is a great way to build the confidence of your students. On this bulletin board, you may not want to just put A papers, but anything the children feel is their very best work regardless of the grade.

71.

Always let students go to the restroom when they ask. You are better safe than sorry.

Sometimes, children are unable to determine ahead of time when they need to go to the restroom and only recognize this when they are about to have an accident. In addition, some students have a lot of constipation issues and need to go and spend a considerable amount of time in the bathroom.

Develop a system to allow students to go that is private and prevents any embarrassment such as a sign-out book with the time and their name (this can prove helpful if there are any behavioral issues in the bathroom because you will have a log as to who went and what time).

Children should be allowed to go when they need to in addition to the regularly scheduled bathroom breaks, but if it is excessive, document the times and contact the parents to make sure there is not a medical issue. You and the parents can determine if the child truly has to use the bathroom or if she is using the break as an avoidance technique to get out of working.

72.

Compliment every child at least once a day. It may be the only compliment some get.

Children thrive on adult attention. It only takes a minute to sincerely compliment a child. Some parents are so very busy and have such hectic lives, they forget how badly children need to feel special, liked, pretty, handsome, smart, etc. Notice small changes like a new haircut or new shoes. Notice nice handwriting or an act of kindness. Make sure you are sincere because children can detect a phony a mile away!

The greatest compliment is if you say something positive about a child to another adult within earshot of the child. That is like your boss telling her boss something good about you. It feels amazing!

73.

Never read a note from one child to another child aloud to the class.

Embarrassment is felt and remembered long after any lesson you were trying to teach the child. A student will feel anything you say or do in front of the class for years whether it is a positive thing or a negative one.

If you retrieve a note a child wrote to another student, simply place it in your desk without opening it. This way, it gives the child the message that you may read it later, but at that moment it is learning time. The child will know it was inappropriate because you collected it and put it away and it is embarrassing enough for them to think you may actually read it. There is never a reason for you to read it in front of anyone.

74.

Always show your students respect. They will return the favor.

If you speak kindly and show caring, concern, and empathy for your students, they will show you the same. If you have to discipline them or correct them, you can say to them, "I'm sorry such a great kid made this choice, but now you will have to accept the consequences for that choice."

Belittling the child or embarrassing the child is not teaching him anything other than that you are an unkind adult.

75.

Never eat in your classroom in front of the children unless they have a snack, too.

This is simply rude. Imagine yourself in a college class that doesn't allow food. It is 9:00 a.m., and you didn't eat breakfast and you are really hungry. During the lecture, the professor takes out a donut and begins eating it. It is a distraction, at the least, and it says, "I can break the rules, but you cannot."

You teach children manners such as sharing and waiting for everyone to be served before eating. Make sure you are always a role model. Make sure you are behaving in such a manner that you want them to emulate.

76.

Act really interested when a child tells you something and let her finish before you continue the lesson. If there is no time, tell her you cannot wait to hear it after class and do not forget.

Many times, you will feel like you simply cannot listen to another story about a pet or about an uncle. These stories make up the lives of these little people and they want desperately to share them. They can pick up any insincerity, boredom, or frustration.

When they tell you something, look in their eyes and nod your head and ask a question about what they said. If you simply do not have time right then to listen, tell them you cannot wait to hear the story and let them know a good time they can share it with you. Tell them a time to come up to your desk to share their news that day and make yourself a note so *you* don't forget!

77.

When they draw a picture for you, let them know how really creative they are and how much you love it.

Hang every picture up in the classroom. Take them down weekly and keep them in a notebook. Kids love to see their work on display and they love to give their teacher special things. These treasures are from their heart. To you, it is a piece of paper with some crayon marks on it—to them, it is a special gift to you.

78.

Never run out of paper, pencils, glue, crayons, folders, and other supplies. Their parents may not have been paid that month.

There are numerous sales on school supplies right around the beginning of October when Halloween decorations go on display and back-to-school sales are over. Stock up on supplies so you can hand them new supplies, nonchalantly, when they run out of them.

Send a note home for the parents to replace worn-out supplies; but if they do not respond, let the child have yours. Everyone feels good when they have new school supplies, and it is not the child's fault if the parents cannot afford to purchase the supplies or if the parents do not take them to the store to buy them. It is worth every penny you will spend.

79.

Give each child a small gift like a pencil or a colorful eraser for holidays. It means the world to them.

With children, it truly is the giving and not the gift. They will be giving you lots of presents and you will want to give them something small to take home or use in school. Sometimes, book order companies will give you extra books each time you make purchases. You can accumulate these books and give them to children at the end of the school year for summer reading or over the winter break. Make sure the gift is not food or food related due to allergies.

80.

On Valentine's Day, every child must bring a Valentine for everyone in the classroom or bring none at all. This way there are no empty Valentine bags.

Give them construction paper to make Valentines. Some cannot afford to buy them. Another idea is to purchase extra boxes of Valentines and have them on hand. At the end of February, you can buy Valentines for up to 90 percent off in most retail stores. Stock up on some girl themes, boy themes, and gender-neutral themes. Let the children choose which they would like if they do not have any on the morning of the Valentine party. They quickly can write their name on each.

81.

Find reasons to put lots of stickers on their papers.

This tells students you have looked at their paper individually and like what you see. It is a tiny boost.

Children of all ages like stickers. My husband teaches engineering to juniors and seniors in high school. He puts stickers on their papers. One time when he ran out, they asked him why their papers were missing stickers!

82.

Learn the students' names as quickly as possible and call them by their preferred names (i.e., Andy instead of Andrew).

I used to have a superintendent who called me Becky instead of Rebecca. I haven't been called Becky since I was a child, but he decided from the time I met him that I was Becky. Before a big district-wide meeting when I knew he was going to introduce me, I told him most people know me as Rebecca and wanted to know if he could introduce me as Rebecca. He was very gracious and said he could and he was so glad I told him that. He did introduce me as Rebecca, but the next time he saw me, he said, "Hi, Becky." It's important to call people what they prefer.

83.

Send a child to the principal's office to report good news like an unexpected "A" on a spelling test or other significant events or improvements.

Principals are not like they used to be. They do not sit in their offices and wait to suspend, paddle, or yell at children. Most are very kind and want students to develop positive relationships with them. You can help foster this relationship by telling the children how excited the principal is going to be to hear all of their good news from the classroom.

Send a quick e-mail to the principal first letting her know you are coming. The principal may even want to stop by your room to congratulate the child. Imagine that child knowing you were saying great things about her to the principal!

84.

Reward your students with homework coupons to allow them to not do or delay a homework assignment.

They can use one if they forget to do it or if their baseball game runs into overtime. Children have issues arise at night just as adults do. Some children may panic when they cannot complete their homework because they do not want to disappoint you and they are afraid of school consequences. They need a way out of this and a way to be able to control the situation.

It can become a lesson in responsibility. This is like a savings account for homework. They will learn quickly that if they use it carelessly, it will not be there for them when they truly need it.

89.

Do not let anyone at school talk about there not being a tooth fairy, Easter Bunny, or Santa Claus.

Many children still believe in these characters until the fifth grade or they are at the "don't ask, don't tell" stage where they pretend they believe. Some children will try to tell others these characters are not real. Stop the conversation immediately and, if they ask you, tell them you believe in everything! Their parents may not want to pop their bubble yet and it is not anyone's responsibility to do it for them.

90.

Don't compare one child to another. It is like comparing apples to oranges.

Do you want them to compare you unfavorably with their other teachers? Children need to compete against themselves, not each other. This is most difficult when you have a child with whom you really connect and you compare that child to a classmate who is somewhat annoying and disruptive. It is always important to put yourself in the child's shoes and imagine what it would feel like if you were compared unfavorably with a colleague. Never pit one against the other, because when you do that, someone always loses.

91.

Give the students a sense of power.

Let them choose what subject you will do first that day or which assignment they would like to do. If you let them choose some things, they will be more accepting of the things you choose.

Routine and consistency are extremely important for children, but so is a sense of control over their environment. Some days, ask them what they would like to do first and why, and then take a vote. This teaches them about voting and "majority rules" but also teaches them you value their opinion and they are an important part of the class.

92.

Even if you have fifty students in your classroom, and you do not think you can accommodate one more, warmly welcome a new student.

Do not make an overcrowded classroom the new student's problem. He has enough to worry about. Make a new student feel welcome by assigning the student a buddy. Choose a student who is well liked and is a positive role model. This makes the role model feel good and gets the student off to the right start.

I have seen teachers argue with the person who is delivering the new student to the classroom by saying the child doesn't belong there and they got the last new student. Many times, this has happened with the classroom door open, so the students in the class hear the teacher complaining, as does the poor new student who is just trying to fit in somewhere.

93.

Each child has a little "magic" in him.

Many of us become so overwhelmed by all of the responsibility, the noise, and the many things we have to get done every day, we forget how wonderful and magical each child is. Regardless of the difficulties you might have with a child, take time to find the magic in him—the unique, wonderful part of him.

An activity I have done in my self-esteem small group counseling sessions is to have the parents list the ten best things about their child. The child is not supposed to see the list, and it is placed in an envelope and sealed until it is handed to me during the next session.

I used to read these silently before letting each child know what they said. I would ask if each child wanted me to read the list aloud to the class (all of them have said yes). Then I would read them to the class and watch the child beam! If a parent had included something a little embarrassing like "He's so cute because he still sleeps with his teddy, Mr. Bojangles," then I would simply skip over that one. I wouldn't say the numbers, but I would just read them in any order so the children wouldn't realize if I read less than ten of them.

94.

Do not allow children to pass out tests or report cards to their classmates.

A child's grades are as confidential as your evaluations. Even if the child has earned straight As, it is not for you to disclose to the class without the child's permission.

Sharing grades of students will make someone feel inferior—either the child whose report card you are reading or the child who is hearing about a classmate who received straight As. The grades are confidential and if a child knows his classmates are aware of his grade, it may lead to embarrassment, not to mention legal issues.

CLASSROOM MANAGEMENT

Teach love, generosity, good manners and some of that will drift from the classroom to the home and who knows, the children will be educating the parents.

—Roger Moore

95.

Plan for more work than the children can possibly do; in elementary school, idle time equals trouble.

Some students will take lots of time to do their work and some will rush right through to finish quickly. Make sure you have a clear list of activities written in a prominent place in your room they can do after their work is complete.

You may even want them to have a packet of fun activities in their desks they can work on that is due at the end of the month. Perhaps the packets can have a month theme such as pumpkin mazes and witch crosswords for October and Valentine activities for February. Of course, these activities need to be curriculum driven and not simply coloring pages.

96.

Absolutely nothing should be on your students' desks when you are teaching. Their attention spans are short.

Students' primary focus should be on you when you are doing direct instruction. Therefore, nothing at all should be on the students' desks such as pencils, rulers, erasers, and so forth. In elementary school, anything can turn into a toy. Make sure even name tags that are taped to their desks are laminated and thoroughly taped down so they do not become a distraction. Throughout the lesson, you may want to remind the students that you need both eyes on your eyes.

97.

Make sure you demand utter silence when the morning announcements are on.

This shows students how important it is to listen to the principal and it shows respect. How can you expect students to listen to you when you do not listen to the principal? During the morning announcements is not the time to take attendance and ask who is buying lunch. The principal's voice is a signal that the day is officially beginning and learning should begin. Students should be calm and in their seats and ready for the day.

If you are talking on the phone or e-mailing or talking to students during this time, it is a signal to the students the principal is not important and the announcements are a waste of time.

98.

Tell your students whenever an adult enters the classroom, they are to be very quiet and on their best behavior. This preparation will save you from many embarrassing moments.

This is a must during the first week of school. Let your students know their behavior is a direct reflection on them, their classmates, and you. Tell them when someone enters the classroom, it is "show time"! Tell them they are to pretend the President of the United States has arrived and they are to stay seated, to work quietly, and not to approach you unless they are bleeding or purple.

Adults in the building will get a good impression when they enter your classroom, and this is a good way to show off your classroom management skills. Maybe you can even let the students earn "manners points" and whenever an adult enters the room or whenever they walk very quietly in the hall as a class, they will get points that can add up to a special surprise like fifteen minutes of free time or extra recess.

99.

A touch on the shoulder and a smile, when the students are working quietly, works wonders.

If a child is getting antsy and is beginning to be distracted, a simple touch on the shoulder usually brings the child back into focus. It also lets the child know you are watching him and wanting him to stay on task, but you are giving him a gentle reminder in a loving way.

100.

As a discipline measure, never tell a child he cannot eat breakfast, snack, or lunch at school. It may be the only meal he gets all day.

Do not ever use food other than for nourishment. Do not use it as a punishment or as a reward. Food should be just a necessity for a healthy body and not have alternative value or power. This power can ultimately lead to eating disorders, hoarding food, overly valuing food, and so on.

101.

Never lose control of your class.

By losing control, you tell them it is acceptable for them to lose control and you may never regain it.

You are the adult. You are the role model. If you try to be your students' friend, you will lose control. You can have fun with them and joke around to a point, but never let it get out of hand. They have friends—they need a positive role model and teacher.

102.

Never use the words "shut up" in your classroom.

"Shut up" means you have lost control. There is never a good time or an appropriate time to tell someone to "shut up." "Shut up" is the other "S" word.

If you are resorting to this, you need to take a serious look at your classroom management strategies. This is telling the students, and your colleagues, you have lost control of yourself and of your students and you need some help. Talk to the school counselor if you feel these situations occur frequently and learn some tips on how to better manage the classroom. This will create a less stressful environment for the students and for you.

103.

Explain distractions to the children so their attention will be on you.

If a maintenance worker or the custodian comes into your room to fix something, explain what is going on. If there is construction going on outside of your window, use it as a lesson in community workers.

104.

Don't reward the children with candy, cookies, etc. Of course, allergies are an issue, but you do not want to teach children to reward themselves with food.

There are many other, better rewards such as pencils, stickers, erasers, free homework passes, lunch with you, extra computer time, and extra recess. Children do not need to get donuts, candy, or cookies.

When I taught Sunday school thirty years ago, I brought donuts for the children as a reward. Each child was given a donut and I turned around to help one of the children. All of a sudden, I saw a little five-year-old boy stuffing three donuts in his mouth. At that moment, his mother entered the classroom. She was shocked and said that was the first time he had ever eaten sugar in his life and didn't even know what it tasted like until that moment. I have to say, that was not my favorite day of Sunday school!

105.

If a child misbehaves, let him write a letter to his parents telling them what he will do next time in the same situation.

If the misbehavior is more severe, have the child call her parents from school and put them on the speakerphone. This will make the child take responsibility for her actions and will let her parents know exactly what the child is admitting to. This way, it is less likely the child will tell another version when she gets home.

106.

Never send a child to the principal's office for bad behavior unless you positively cannot control the child's behavior and you have tried everything.

Of course, if the behavior may result in a suspension, such as the child having a weapon or physically hurting another person, then let the principal know immediately.

You want to be known as the person who can handle most anything. The principal has hundreds of students to deal with and you want to make the principal's life as easy as possible. When you do seek the principal's help, she will know you truly need help if it doesn't happen very often.

107.

Never, ever, ever touch a child in anger!

When you lose your temper, you have lost. When you touch a child in anger, you have made a career-ending mistake.

108.

Quietly walk your children through a fire drill, tornado drill, lock-down drill, etc., even before the principal has the first one of the year.

Come back to the classroom and talk about it. Make sure your children know these things are very rare, but you need to be prepared so everyone can be safe. Never roll your eyes at the sound of a fire drill or act like you are annoyed to be interrupted. Show the children you take the drill seriously, just as they should.

Make sure your children are *completely* quiet during these drills. It is a universal school rule and it is for the safety of all. You do not want other teachers to correct your children! That can be quite embarrassing for a new teacher.

109.

Always be consistent and have a routine.

Children need routine and thrive on it. Every day should be structured the same way, and the children should know what to expect. Children who feel out of control and feel they do not know what is coming next begin to panic and act out by trying to gain attention or by losing control of their emotions. When things are consistent, children feel safe and calm. Then, when something unexpected happens, they will feel safe enough to cope with the change if you are calm.

110.

Send no more than two students at a time to the restroom. It will save you many headaches.

Children will be children and they like to socialize and have fun. What better place to have fun than away from the teacher's eyes with water and bathroom humor? Kids get into trouble in the bathroom. Have a bathroom log. Each child can sign out before they go and, when they return, another can go. Having a log is important so you can see if anyone is abusing the privilege or if there is a pattern of when a child needs to go every day due to a medical issue or to avoid a particular subject in school.

111.

Don't let the students get out of their seats without permission. This can be the quickest way to chaos.

Depending on your tolerance level and the group of students you have, you can allow students to get up to get a tissue or sharpen a pencil, but it can easily get out of hand. Children need to raise their hand before getting out of their seat, however you can have some exceptions such as when you are reading with small groups of children or when students are doing centers or need to turn in papers.

It may be you can start out the year stricter and ease up when the children can handle themselves. I have been in classrooms where children are all doing something different and some are working while others are walking to a center, others are turning in papers, and others are quietly working. This classroom looked like a small city that was running effectively and efficiently with everyone knowing exactly what to do and when to do it.

Conversely, I have seen classrooms where children are talking, interrupting others' learning, getting out of their seats, leaving the classroom and going to the bathroom, and so on. This is chaotic and not a good learning environment at all.

MEDIA, SOCIAL MEDIA, AND COMPUTERS

It's all about people. It's about networking and being nice to people and not burning any bridges.

—Mike Davidson

112.

Be very careful with social networking.

Social networking can be very dangerous for a teacher. If you are in any pictures holding alcohol or you talk about your job or students, it could be career ending. Is this fair? Maybe not, but it is reality. I have heard fellow educators discuss children in their classes and not mention their names, but any parent or school employee would know whom they are talking about. I have heard teachers talk about how hard their class is or how they need a drink after a hard week. These things are unprofessional and can get you into trouble. If you do decide to do social networking, make sure you *never* friend a parent or a student! Even though you may not post pictures, someone may tag you in a picture and show you doing something you don't want people to see.

113.

Do not e-mail children directly.

When children are not in your classroom, any correspondence needs to go through their parents. The only exceptions to this rule would be if you mail them a card at their home to welcome them into your class at the beginning of the school year, you wish them a happy summer at the end of the school year, you thank them for a gift, or you send them a get-well card after a long illness. You may want to write "In care of" and then the parents' names on the envelope.

114.

Do not go on the computer with your class sitting around the computer looking at the screen unless you are completely sure there are no inappropriate pop-up advertisements.

Go to the site by yourself before you invite the class to look at the screen so there are no surprises. Being prepared is key when using the computer and school-related websites. Any type of media needs to be reviewed first such as DVDs, websites, CDs, and even radio stations.

115.

Do not shop or go on social networking sites from your school computer, whether it is your planning time or not.

School districts can track what sites you have visited on your computer, and you do not want to have to explain why you are using school time for leisure activities. Remember, social networking sites show when a message was posted by displaying how many minutes or hours have gone by since you posted the message. Therefore, if it says you posted a message two hours prior and that was during school time, it is obvious you are not teaching, but you are socializing.

116.

Print out every e-mail you receive from a parent and put them in a folder designated for each child.

That communication is vital; you may need those e-mails later to remind parents how much you have communicated with them and strategies you have tried or suggested they try at home. You will be surprised when a parent calls the principal to say you have not been letting them know their child is failing a subject. When you pull out that child's file from your desk and show all of the parent contact you have had, the parents and the child suddenly have to take responsibility and the blame is off you. Make sure these e-mails are in a personal file in your classroom and do not go in the child's cumulative folder in the main office. Keep these files for at least a year after the child has moved on to the next grade.

117.

When parents e-mail you throughout the day, set boundaries.

Do not e-mail them back right away because they may expect this and become annoyed if you wait until after school or the next school day. At orientation, explain to the parents you are busy teaching their children during the day and may not be able to answer their phone calls or e-mails right away, but you will do your best. Tell them you will return their e-mail or call within twenty-four hours and make sure you do.

118.

Do not contact the media for any reason on your own.

Some teachers feel a need to promote themselves by calling their local newspaper to tell them about a great project their students are doing. The problem is, the reporter may be critical of your project or may misinterpret the goal of your lesson and express this in the newspaper. It could completely backfire.

This is the same with writing an editorial in your local paper. You are a representative of your school district, and they want to control which stories are reported and what information goes out into the community.

If you have an exciting project you want to share, write a small summary and highlight the work the students are doing. E-mail this to your principal. Colorful pictures also can be included in the e-mail showing the students actively participating in the activity (make sure you have parental permission before using a picture of a specific child). Some districts have a Director of Public Relations, but do not forward anything to that person without consulting your principal first.

119.

Do not assume all parents want their child's name in lights!

Many school districts have a release form for parents to fill out at the beginning of the school year to give permission for their child to be photographed or videotaped. Some parents do not mind this at all while others feel it is an invasion of privacy. Some children are estranged from one of their parents and the custodial parent does not want the child's face on the Internet, in photographs, or on television for safety reasons. Therefore, always get a signed release from the parents before sharing these photos or DVDs.

120.

Be careful around reporters.

If you are at a school event and a local reporter from the newspaper or a local television station is there, watch what you say. It may seem very helpful to share information about the special event or the school. It may seem like you are helping promote the event organizers and the school district.

Some reporters have a way of getting more information than the person meant to share. They may ask a question about how the wonderful event was started and then ask how it was paid for since the district is running out of money. A central office representative, a Director of Public Relations, or the school principal can better answer these questions. It is always safe to simply stay away from situations such as these.

HOMEWORK

The same people who never did their homework
in high school are still doing that to this very day
out in the real world.

—Jules Shear

121.

Follow your district's homework policy.

Many districts have their own homework policies. Look in the student handbook to find out what your district's policy is. Make sure you follow it to the letter, because homework can be a controversial issue among parents, administrators, and teachers. Some parents hate it and others demand it; some teachers swear by it and others think it is a waste of time. Despite what you think, follow what the district handbook says.

122.

Make sure homework is meaningful.

Homework should not be busywork or coloring. Homework should be practicing skills students have been taught at school. It can be a review of a concept like nouns and verbs or used as practice such as for math facts. Children can practice research skills at home on the computer or practice study skills.

123.

During orientation, make it clear to parents what the school's homework policy is and make your expectations clear.

Parents should know what is expected of their children at home and what is expected of them as parents. Make it clear they are not to do their child's homework, but they are expected to be available if their child has questions. Some teachers find it helpful to use the Rule of Three where a child can ask three questions per assignment. The child has to make sure the questions are important because they will run out quickly. The parent can give the child three paperclips per assignment, and the child has to relinquish one each time she asks a question. When the paperclips are gone, the child is on her own. As the child gets older, this rule changes to three per evening. This rule can be especially effective for children who depend on their parents to do their homework for them or expect their parents to sit right beside them and guide them through every question.

124.

Reading should always be included in homework.

Many teachers of young children have the parents fill out a nightly reading log. The parent writes the name of the book read or the minutes read and then signs their name. The children bring this log back to their teacher each day for the teacher to put a sticker or smiley face on the log. As they get older, the children may be expected to just read for twenty minutes every night on their own.

Limited required reading is always a safe bet when it comes to homework assignments. Every child in elementary school needs the practice and this is good training for them for middle school, high school, and college when the reading load is compounded.

125.

Make sure students know you are looking at their homework and you value their time spent at home doing it.

Some teachers expect homework and then never check it or even look at it. Make sure the students get some type of feedback for doing the work. It may not be that you want to give a grade for each assignment, but at least collect the homework and put a comment, a check mark, or a sticker on the paper.

Have you ever been required to do work and then your boss or teacher doesn't even know whether you completed it? It makes you think they don't really care, and so you don't, either.

126.

Make the amount of homework fit the age of the student.

If your district does not have a homework policy, ask three veteran teachers how much homework they give on a daily basis. Ask your teammates in your grade, but also ask someone in a grade below you and a grade above. This will give you an idea of what other teachers expect of their students.

Some teachers use the simple policy of assigning ten minutes a grade, for example, kindergartners get ten minutes, first graders get fifteen minutes, second graders get twenty minutes, and so on.

Some teachers make a packet with a calendar on the front page that has an assignment listed on each day. In the packet are worksheets that correspond with each calendar date. On each day of the month (Monday through Friday), there is a simple practice assignment such as measure how many inches your refrigerator is or write five words that rhyme with cat. This packet is handed out at the beginning of the month and is due on the last day of the month.

127.

Make it easy for a child to complete their homework at home.

A child may have a chaotic home life. There may not be much supervision due to parents having more than one job and/or being single. There may be many siblings and no quiet place to work.

If a child consistently is not bringing in homework, speak with the child privately and ask him how you can help. Ask the child if it would help for you to give him a special homework bag with scissors, crayons, sharpened pencils, paper, and such to take home to keep. Explain to the child that he can put this homework bag in a special place in his room to get out whenever he needs to work on homework. Explain that he needs to pretend to have an office where it is quiet and he has all of his supplies. Tell him to put the supplies back in the bag every time he finishes his homework and leave it in a safe spot out of the way of younger siblings and pets. In the bag, you may want to add flashcards, sight words, and other helpful homework supplies. Sometimes, teachers assume homework is not being turned in due to laziness or noncompliance when, in reality, it is the home environment and somewhat out of the child's control. Help the child gain control.

POSITIVE LEARNING ENVIRONMENT

Education is not the filling of a pail, but the lighting of a fire.

—William Butler Yeats

128.

Play calming music during difficult lessons.

Learning a new concept is very stressful for anyone. The environment in which you learn a new concept is crucial in your ability to accept and understand the information. Pretend you are learning a new language. If the classroom is noisy, in disarray, and different people around you are doing their own thing while you are trying to concentrate, you can imagine how difficult it would be. Now imagine yourself in a quiet room where soft, instrumental music is playing in the background and everyone is focused and on task. What a better way to learn!

129.

Play holiday (nonreligious) music before school during the month of December when students are getting settled.

This seems like such a small thing, but kids are so excited around this time of year and are usually indoors a lot due to weather. They need a little jump start to be motivated to come to school. This is a small thing, but it makes the day begin on a brighter note.

130.

Collect lots of red and green construction paper for winter holiday, Valentine's Day, and St. Patrick's Day activities. In some schools, art supplies are hard to come by.

Many schools in the country are having severe financial problems. Sometimes, it is first come first served when it comes to supplies. Leave enough for your colleagues, of course, but remember to think ahead when choosing even though it is just August. Also, after the back-to-school rush, many discount chains have great sales on school supplies. Sometimes items like folders, crayons, pencils, construction paper, tape, and glue are up to 90 percent off. Always be on the lookout for supplies in case you run out or if a child cannot afford to bring supplies to school. Children will be more apt to want to learn and will take more pride in their learning if they have their very own supplies with their names on them.

131.

The classroom is the children's home away from home.

Always keep it clean and orderly. Always make sure it is warm, safe, and inviting. Chaos leads to chaos. If your classroom is messy, has clutter all over it, and is overly stimulating, or if it is trashy and in disarray, it is not a good learning environment for children. If it looks like a stark, white, hospital room, it is not a good environment, either. Your classroom should be colorful and pleasant to the eye. You should have designated areas for specific activities such as a reading corner that would make anyone want to curl up with a good book. You may want to have an art center where you keep all of your art supplies in nice, neat containers and bins that are labeled. Order is essential in a classroom. Children need to know exactly where to go to find what they need, and it needs to be in the same place every time. Adding things like plants, curtains, and pictures of your family can create a homey atmosphere that is warm and relaxing to the children.

132.

Take the children outside at least once a week for a brisk walk or to read under a tree.

Changes in the learning environment help all of us learn more easily and effectively. Ever worked in an office *with* windows versus without? Ever ride in a convertible? Sometimes, fresh air and nature are needed to relax children. Will they be distracted if you are reading a story outside? Sure they will, but the change of pace and fresh air are good for all of you.

133.

Begin each lesson with a smile and tell them something to get them excited about it.

We learn better and retain longer if we have a reason to learn material. Before each lesson, try to hook them and give them a reason to learn. Do this by telling a funny joke or story pertaining to the lesson or bring in something interesting to share. For example, I was teaching third grade. We were going to write a fantasy story in language arts. I happened to wear a big and unusual-looking ring to school that day and I told them the ring was magic. I told them if I touched their paper, wonderful ideas would spill out of their pencils. This simple tactic got them excited to write. This is much better than saying, "Okay, get out a piece of paper . . ."

134.

At the beginning of each day, stand at the door and tell each child how glad you are to see him or her.

I had a principal, Mrs. Bender, who stood at the front door of the school every morning and greeted each child with, "Have a great day of learning," or "I'm glad you are here today," or "Thank you for coming." The children loved this and gave her many hugs and high-fives to begin their day. One kindergartner named Allison told me Mrs. Bender was her best friend. I asked her how she knew that and she said, "Because she hugs me every morning!"

135.

Once a day, read a good book aloud to the children and all of you sit on the floor.

There are so many wonderful books kids will look forward to hearing each day! A few examples are: *There's a Boy in the Girl's Bathroom* and *Rules*. Children like to have a routine and if, after lunch every day, they sit quietly and listen to a story, it calms then down enough to learn in the afternoon. Also, this close time with you and their friends on the floor feels warm and cozy like a family.

136.

Let the students have pen pals from another classroom.

They can write to them once a week and plan a special day to meet them at the end of the semester. This activity is great for developing writing skills and social skills. It is fun to have your kids write to an older grade or younger grade and have them tell the other class what to expect in that grade and tips for learning in that grade. At the end of the semester, they can have lunch together or plan a special poetry reading, for example.

137.

Eat lunch with your students at least once a month in the classroom or under a tree and do not talk about schoolwork.

This is a good time to learn about your students. Are they upset about a bully? Are they having difficulty at home? Many teachers refer students to the school counselor after some of these lunches because they learn the child needs some support and they would not have become aware of this if they hadn't had such a relaxed conversation over lunch.

Children will learn better if they can relate to you and you to them. Develop a rapport with your students and they will be more apt to perform well for you.

138.

Don't show a video or play a song in your classroom unless you have thoroughly reviewed it beforehand and, of course, make sure it is tied to the curriculum.

I have known even experienced teachers who have not done this and curse words pop up in the movie. Children love to tell their parents when they hear a swearword. Previewing these movies will prevent parent phone calls. In addition, do not show a PG movie without parent permission. G movies are okay, but a movie that suggests parental guidance needs it.

139.

Be honest.

If you did not sleep well the night before, tell your students. You would be surprised at how sympathetic they can be. Your honesty adds to your humanity and makes you a much more effective role model.

I had a full day of guidance classes to get through the day after my beloved dog, Chance, died. I had not slept and was having a rough time. I decided to tell the students this. They were amazing! We talked about it, they drew pictures and wrote letters for me, and they helped me through the day. For days after this, children would come up and ask me how I was doing or tell me about their pet dying and how it affected them. This honest disclosure helped the children see I was human and I was very sad, but I could get through it with a little help from my friends.

140.

Relate all lessons to the children's own experiences. This will keep their interest.

If you are at a conference and the lecturer relates the content to biotechnology or entomology, you may not be as interested in the lecture as you would be if it related to elementary education or a special interest or television show you liked. You want to be a part of the lessons and understand them. So do the children in your class.

141.

Show the children pictures of your family and your pets.

Let them know you do have a life after school just as they do. Children love to hear about your personal life so they can relate to you. Keep in mind they too have a very different and separate life outside the classroom.

Remember, some children love to talk about their home experiences, but others want to come to school because it is safe and constant. If a child doesn't talk about home much, it may be because she doesn't want to share things that are sad or uncomfortable or she simply wants to forget about it during the school day. Don't press the issue or make her talk about it. Just let her know you are there for her if she chooses to.

142.

Get paper plates, napkins, and plastic utensils and take your children into the cafeteria to teach them table manners. It will be a lesson they will thank you for in years to come.

Some children never learn any table manners at home. I have seen fifth-graders who eat like toddlers; it is very sad because other students notice, but the fifth-grader really doesn't know what he is doing wrong.

You may also teach them little tricks like the fork goes on the left and the spoon and knife on the right. (Trick: The word *fork* has four letters and so does the word *left*. The words *spoon* and *knife* each have five letters and so does the word *right*.)

143.

Be extra cheery on Mondays. You do not know what kind of weekend the children have had.

I know it is very difficult to get up on Mondays and feel cheery sometimes. Kids feel the same way and by third grade they realize they are made to do this every day and it is a lot of work. They know they don't have a choice. If they are struggling in school or have trouble with friends, they don't want to come at all some mornings. If they enter the classroom and feel you are happy to see them and in a good mood, it can only boost their mood and prepare them for their week of learning.

144.

Help children enter your classroom with a smile on their faces each day.

Stand at the door and ask them one great thing that they hope happens that day in school. It may be that they get to play outside, write on the board, or sit by a friend. Tell them you are so glad they are there that day.

145.

Help children leave your classroom with a smile on their faces each day.

Stand at the door and tell them good-bye every day and ask them if they want a hug or a handshake good-bye. Ask them one great thing about their day before they leave the classroom. Give them a quick compliment such as, "You worked really hard today."

146.

Have a comfortable reading corner in your classroom and include a rocking chair, stuffed animals, and other comfy things.

School is the children's home away from home. They need to have a relaxing place to be calm and feel safe and cozy if they are having a bad day or if they need to relax. Teach them that reading is a wonderful and relaxing "vacation" where they can just escape. It will be a lifelong lesson they will cherish.

147.

On occasion, let the children bring slippers or comfy socks to class and, during a hard lesson or test, let them put them on.

This is an easy way to get them to work harder when you let them know you realize something you are teaching may be challenging. This simple thing is fun and lets them know you have empathy for them and you understand the lesson may be difficult.

148.

Always have a positive attitude.

That is something your students will never forget. If you are smiling and positive, they will be, too. If you are grumpy and irritated most of the time, they will be, too.

Children can tell you immediately who loves their job at school and who does not. I heard one child say, "If that teacher is so grumpy all the time, why doesn't she just stay home until she is happy?" Exactly.

149.

Children learn best when they are laughing.

A child who is laughing is not a guarded, defensive, or frightened child. Relaxed, laughing children can learn more readily and more rapidly. Keep them laughing by telling jokes, reading funny stories, telling them funny things that happened to you as a child, etc.

There is a big difference between being light and funny and being silly and unprofessional. Saying crude things about bathrooms or bodily functions will definitely elicit a laugh, but they are totally unprofessional. Being extremely silly may result in losing classroom control, so be careful with humor. Cynicism and sarcasm are never acceptable. Young children do not understand it and many times these techniques are used to cut down or make fun of someone.

150.

Have fun and smile a lot.

When you are smiling, you are communicating that you are in control and that all is well with the world—not only are you telling this to the children, but you are also telling yourself. You got into this business for the children and because you love children and are great with them! Now show them!

ABOUT THE AUTHOR

Rebecca C. Schmidt has worked in elementary education for twenty-three years as a teacher and a school counselor. She has published books to help children cope with difficult life situations. Some of her books include *My Book about Cancer*; *Why Would Someone Want to Die?*; *65 Interactive Healing Activities to Guide Children through the Grieving Process*; and *Counselor Pages*, a book and CD with ideas to help counselors make their lives easier. Mrs. Schmidt will be featured as "Author of the Month" in an upcoming ePIC Internet newsletter.

Rebecca works and lives in Mayfield Heights, Ohio, with her husband, Craig, and her two daughters, Hannah and Lauren.